Exploring tough questions facing youth today

SALT, LIGHT, AND THE GOOD LIFE

Blessings and the Sermon on the Mount

The Pastoral Center

ISBN 978-1-949628-06-7
Printed in the United States of America.
10 9 8 7 6 5 4 3 2 1   22 21 20 19

Published by The Pastoral Center, http://pastoral.center.

Developed in partnership with MennoMedia and Brethren Press. Series editors: Fumiaki Tosu, Ann Naffziger, and Paul Canavese. *Salt, Light, and the Good Life*: Writers, Charles Kwon, Peter Bergeron, and Lani Wright. Project editor, Lani Wright. Staff editors, Susan E. Janzen, Julie Garber, and James Deaton. Updated design, Paul Stocksdale.

All rights reserved. Purchase of this book includes a license to reproduce this resource for use in a single parish, school, or other similar organization. You are allowed to share and make unlimited copies only for use within the organization that licensed it. If you serve more than one organization, each should purchase its own license. You may not post this document to any web site without explicit permission to do so. Outside of these conditions, no part of this book may be reproduced in any form or by any means, electronic or mechanical, including photocopying, recording, taping, or via any retrieval system, without the written permission of The Pastoral Center, 1212 Versailles Ave., Alameda, CA 94501. Thank you for cooperating with our honor system regarding our licenses.

For questions or to order additional copies or licenses, please call 1-844-727-8672 or visit http://pastoral.center.

Portions of this work © 2019 by The Pastoral Center / PastoralCenter.com. Adapted and published with permission from Generation Why Bible Studies. © 1997, 2015 Brethren Press, Elgin, IL 60120 and MennoMedia, Harrisonburg, VA 22803, U.S.A. All rights reserved.

Unless otherwise noted, the Scripture passages contained herein are from the *New Revised Standard Version of the Bible*, copyright © 1989 by the National Council of the Churches of Christ in the United States of America. Used by permission. All rights reserved.

Bible-based Explorations of Issues Facing Youth

» OVERVIEW

When conversing online, the acronym IRL stands for "in real life." The virtual world of social media, text chats, blogs, and more have the power to remove us from the real world. What we experience online can skew our perspective on what it means to be human. It can numb us, incite us, distract us, depress us, confuse us, and make us rude or impatient. Strangely, this supposedly "social" and "connected" technology can profoundly disconnect us from others.

Religious faith can also place us in a bubble, especially when it distances us from others. When we keep the prophetic message at a safe distance, obscured in theological language and abstractions, we are missing the whole point. And when we see our parish as an insider club that serves itself, we can forget the radically inclusive message entrusted to us: God's love is for *everyone*, and God expects us to transform the *whole world* through that love.

Through the incarnation, God showed up in the real world to show us that our faith is not just about talking the talk, but also walking the walk. It can be risky. It can be confusing. It can hurt. But living out our faith can also bring us great purpose, peace, and joy.

This series connects the Bible with the tough questions that youth (and adults) encounter in their neighborhood, in school, among friends, and even online. This process will help you as a leader break open these issues in a fun and meaningful way, sparking conversation and the kind of life change Jesus invites us to embrace.

» THE ROLE OF PARENTS

As children enter middle school and high school, they become more independent, self-reliant, and, well, self-centered. This can bring parents to make assumptions that this is the time to step back, giving their child more space to form their identity. While there is truth to that at some level (adolescents definitely shouldn't be smothered), this is a stage of life when parents should in fact *lean in*. The apparent confidence and bluster youth show on the outside can mask the insecurity and confusion on the inside. Youth need their parents to be involved more than ever.

» WHOLE FAMILY FORMATION

Parents are the primary teachers of their own children, and parishes are waking up to the fact that faith formation programs need to bring parents into the process if they hope to see faith passed on to the next generation. Recent studies give us more and more evidence that the role of parents is the most important factor in determining whether a child will embrace faith as they move toward adulthood. Research from the Center for the Applied Research on the Apostolate shows that parents who talk about their faith and show through their actions that their faith is important to them are more likely to have children who remain Catholic.

More about Whole Family Formation

To learn more about how your parish can take a comprehensive whole family approach to faith formation, visit **GrowingUpCatholic.com**.

While whole family events with elementary-aged children are on the rise, the role of parents can be an afterthought in youth ministry. We have designed the sessions in this series to work with or without parents present, and we encourage you to offer them as parent-child events.

If you choose to involve parents, it is important to consider before each session how to best do so. Many of the activities in this series are high-energy, creative, or silly. Some parents may need some encouragement to get out of their heads and have fun with the group. A few activities involving physical contact would be inappropriate for parents and youth to participate together, and we have noted them as such.

There are a number of ways to approach discussions with parent participation. Unless you have a small group, you will likely want to break into smaller groups for conversation. Some youth may be self-conscious and unable to be completely honest and open in a group situation with a parent present. For this reason, you may choose in some cases to assign parents to different groups from their own children, or to have separate parent and child groups altogether. Be sure to cover expectations around confidentiality. It is inappropriate for a parent (or youth) to share with another parent what their child said in a small group.

Note that even if parents and their children do not share all conversations together in the session, they will still have a valuable shared experience and can have extended conversations about it later.

THANK YOU

The role you play in gathering, animating, praying with, and forming youth is a valuable one. Thank you for all you do to serve the church and its families!

Bible-based Explorations of Issues Facing Youth

SALT, LIGHT, AND THE GOOD LIFE
Blessings and the Sermon on the Mount

INTRODUCTION

There's a story about a man who preached a sermon that agitated his congregation so much that some walked out in the middle of the service. Others threatened to leave the church if the preacher persisted in such radical talk. Others felt the sermon had some merit, but they cautioned him about straying too far from the "biblical" preaching they expected. A few pumped his hand afterwards, saying it was his best sermon yet.

The preacher was chagrined. Harried and out of time on Saturday night, he'd pulled out an old sermon to preach, and it wasn't even his. He'd preached Jesus' Sermon on the Mount, nearly word for word.

Granted, the Sermon on the Mount doesn't exactly qualify as your conventional 21st-century sermon. In no-holds-barred language, it calls people to radical discipleship. Yet the Sermon is more than a set of high standards preached by an itinerate rabbi years ago; it points to a highly disciplined—and rewarding—way of living, and the "blessings" foretell what anyone can expect as a disciple of Jesus.

Though there have been numerous schemes for organizing the Sermon on the Mount, this study will look at it in four main sections: (1) Beatitudes/Blessings, (2) Salt and Light, (3) Jesus and the Law, and (4) Heavenly Teachings.

BEATITUDES/BLESSINGS

If any of Jesus' disciples had lived to rocking-chair age, they might have regaled their grandkids with "My road of discipleship began on a rocky hill listening to the great Preacher...". The first part of Jesus' Sermon on the Mount is where the disciples started their preparation for a life of discipleship. Jesus lays out the conditions and characteristics he expects his disciples to experience and develop in the course of following him. Though the conditions might tax the spirit, and the rocks in the road of discipleship may loom as boulders, there are also significant rewards.

Preparation Alert

The first four sessions offer an option for **memory work**—strategies for your group to memorize the Blessings and other brief verses of the Sermon. If you choose this, offer consistent reinforcement over the four sessions. You will need index cards and a chalkboard, newsprint, or a screen and electronic device, depending on the option.

EXTENDER SESSION

Extender sessions suggest special activities related to the issue of the unit. They help accommodate the diversity of parish schedules. Since each unit is undated, youth may study units in their entirety and still participate in special events of the parish that get scheduled simultaneously with youth group time. Extender sessions can be used anytime, but the one for this unit best follows **Session 6**. Calculate now whether or not you will be using the extender session.

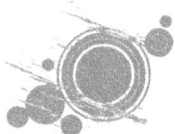

A perspective that might help us personally experience the Beatitudes (or Blessings) is to link each one to the development stages of discipleship: (1) conversion, (2) preparation, and (3) ministry. For example, the first three conditions—poor in spirit, those who mourn, and the meek—are typically experienced *before* one chooses to follow Jesus (conversion). The blessings promised—the reign of heaven, being comforted, and inheritance of the earth—are gifts many experience as they enter God's service. In essence, the Beatitudes are the "Cliff Notes" for becoming a disciple of Christ. Thus, the unit combines the Beatitudes so as to highlight three attitudes that interweave to make room for faith: openness, spiritual discipline, and action.

SALT AND LIGHT

After the Beatitudes/Blessings, there is a brief section of earthy metaphors (5:13-16). Jesus says that disciples are to be the ingredient (salt) that gives life flavor. But like all flavoring, it isn't worth much if it can't be tasted. If the disciples lose their "saltiness," they are of little use. He encourages them to be prominent and active with their witnessing and ministry, so that people will notice God's activity in their midst.

JESUS AND THE LAW

The section on Jesus and the Law (5:17-48) focuses on teaching the essence of God's law. Jesus meant to recover the laws of Moses for their original intent, demanding that biblical laws be rooted in love. He demonstrated to his disciples that it is not simply what we do or say in worship, but what we do in our daily lives that determines how well we are abiding by these laws. Putting a radical twist on teachings about divorce, retaliation, and our attitude toward enemies, Jesus teaches disciples to infuse compassion, grace, and mercy where the letter of the law fails to do so.

HEAVENLY TEACHINGS

In the conclusion of the Sermon on the Mount, Jesus contrasts heavenly and worldly perspectives on religiosity, daily needs and security, and a disciple's journey to the realm of heaven (6:1–7:29).

He teaches disciples to perform religious acts for *God*, not for public recognition, and reminds us God will take care of our needs. Jesus encourages us to ask for whatever we lack, and models prayer life in the Lord's Prayer.

TEACHINGS TO EXPERIENCE AND LIVE BY

Clearly, the teachings of the Sermon on the Mount are radical, both in their simplicity, and in the difficulty of living them as our guide on the Jesus Way. It's a bit like the ice cream called rocky road; this path of discipleship can be rocky, but it's a sweet way to live.

 THE SESSION PLAN: The parts of the session guide

- **Faith story.** The session is rooted in this Bible passage.
- **Faith focus.** The story of the passage in a nutshell.
- **Session goal.** The entire session is built around this goal. What changes—in knowledge, attitude, and/or action—do you desire in your group?
- **Materials needed and advance preparation.** This is what you will need if the session is to go smoothly. You'll feel more at ease if you've taken care of these details before you meet your group.

›› FROM LIFE TO BIBLE TO LIFE

The teaching plan is called *life-centered*. However, when we write each session, we always begin with scripture. We ask, what does this particular passage say, especially to youth? Each session moves from life to Bible to life. So the Bible is really at the center of this way of teaching.

In every session we try to hit upon a tough question participants might ask. Find out what questions on this issue are important for *your* group. By all means, bring your own input and invite your group members to add their own experiences.

›› TEACHING THE SESSION

The five step-by-step movements will carry you from *life to the Bible and back to life*. Each session takes about 45 to 50 minutes. If there is a handout sheet for the session, take note of any complementary activities and stories.

1. **Focus.** Intended to create a friendly climate within the group and to *draw attention* to the issue.

2. **Connect.** Invites participants to *express* their own life experience about the issue, through talking, drawing, role playing, and other activities. Also uses memory, reason, or imagination to get the group thinking about *why* they view the issue the way they do.

3. **Explore the Bible.** What does the Bible *say* about the issue? With a minimum of lecturing, dig into the faith story and search for answers to questions raised in the first activities. The Insights from Scripture section will help clarify the faith story. Help participants discover how the faith community understands the Bible passage.

4. **Apply** the faith story. What does the Bible passage *mean* for contemporary life? This is the "aha!" moment when participants realize the faith story has wisdom for *their* lives.

5. **Respond.** Why does the Bible passage *matter*? What will the group do about the issue in light of what they have learned from their own experiences set alongside the faith story? How can we live the faith story rather than pass it off as a mere intellectual exercise?

›› LOOK AHEAD

Here are reminders for what you need to do for the next session or two.

›› INSIGHTS FROM SCRIPTURE

Here is a resource for Explore the Bible. Don't try to use all the material given. Take what you need to lead the session and answer questions your group may have. Let the Insights section inspire you to think and study more about the passage for the session.

›› HANDOUT SHEETS

Occasionally, there will be a handout sheet to complement your session. If you choose to use this, make enough copies for the group in advance of the session. These sheets may include questions, stories, agree/disagree exercises, charts, pictures, and other materials to stimulate thinking and discussion.

Generally, no participant preparation is required unless the session plan calls for you to contact selected group members for specific tasks.

>>> **SESSION 1**

THE BLESSINGS– INVITATION/CONVERSION >>>

>> KEY VERSE

"Blessed are the poor in spirit, for theirs is the kingdom of heaven." (Matthew 5:3)

>> FAITH STORY

Matthew 5:1-5

>> FAITH FOCUS

Jesus starts the instruction of the disciples by highlighting how they can "enjoy the bliss of heaven"—these are the Blessings (aka the Beatitudes). The message is, if you feel *hopeless* (v. 3), *full of sadness* (v. 4), *beaten down or crushed* (v. 5), Jesus invites you to come to him for nurture, love, and the reward of a relationship with God. These three qualities—poverty of spirit, mourning, and meekness—tend to be preconditions for conversion. People who experience life this way are ripe for a relationship with God. The Beatitudes offer Jesus' understanding, which says, in essence, you *can* go through it and come out blessed on the other end.

>> SESSION GOAL

Assure participants who may be feeling inadequate and/or awkward spiritually that these conditions—poverty of spirit, mourning, and meekness—are exactly the ones that make them receptive to a relationship with God.

>> Materials needed and advance preparation

- A folded invitation for each group member, envelopes for each invitation (see Focus for how to prepare them)
- Index cards and chalkboard/chalk or newsprint/markers, depending on the option (memory work in Explore)
- A variety of Bibles, different versions
- Copies of the handout sheets for Session 1
- Pens/pencils

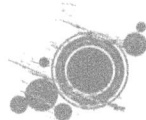 # TEACHING PLAN

1. FOCUS 3 minutes

Before the session, make invitations for each of the participants. Write on the outside fold of each invitation *one* of the following "Uninviting Invitations":

- If You are Poor, You are Invited to...
- If You Feel Sad, You are Invited to...
- If You Feel Beaten Down, You are Invited to...
- If You Feel Hopeless, You are Invited to...
- If You Feel Rejected, You are Invited to...
- If You are Peaceful and Gentle, You are Invited to...

In Real Life | Salt, Light, and the Good Life   7

- If You are Wealthy, You are Invited to...
- If You are Beautiful, You are Invited to...
- If You are Happy, You are Invited to...

Leave the inside blank. Seal the invitations in envelopes, and place them on each seat before the participants arrive or pass them out once everyone is together. Instruct participants not to open the invitation until you give them the go-ahead to read their invitation silently.

2. CONNECT 7 minutes

Now, one by one, invite participants to share what was stated on the outer fold of their invitation. Immediately follow that with the question: *What did you expect to be invited to?*

If the question catches them off guard and they do not have a response, ask them to think for a moment about what they would likely be invited to, given the condition on the card. Ask other members of the group to read their invitations and share what they expected to be invited to. Press them for reasons why. Then ask: *Have you ever been invited to be a part of something because you either had or lacked one of these characteristics?*

3. EXPLORE THE BIBLE 18 minutes

Shift to this activity: *Usually when you get an invitation, you get asked based on certain qualifications or characteristics, or because of who you know. Jesus lays out some unusual qualifications in the invitation to be part of God's crowd.*

> **Option: Memory work.** The Beatitudes are short, and important. Consider having participants memorize them, a few verses at a time, over the next three sessions. Choose one or more of the methods below (some may work better in certain groups than in others), or devise your own. Work in pairs, individually, or in teams.
>
> - Write out the memory verses on a sheet of paper or chalkboard, and say the words together. Repeat, but this time cover or erase some of the words. With each repetition, cover or erase more words, until everyone is saying the words from memory. In the following session, recite together to reinforce.
>
> - Divide into teams of two or more, and give teams a few minutes to memorize the passage or verse together. Then call everyone together and have the first team try to recite the verse(s) from memory. If they can do it, they may sit down. If not, go on to the next team. Keep going around until each team is sitting down.
>
> - Write each word on a separate index card. Have the group members gather around a table or bare spot on the floor. Shuffle the cards and have the group arrange them in the correct order. (For a longer passage, write two or three words on each card. With a larger group, create two or more sets of cards and have subgroups work at separate tables. They can even race to see which group solves the "puzzle" first.) This is a method to use in conjunction with another, since it alone doesn't bring mastery of the verse.
>
> - After initial familiarity with the verse, go around the group having the first person say the first word of the verse, the second person say the second word, etc., through the end of the verse. Then repeat, starting with a different person. After a few trips around the circle, have each person say two words. Then repeat the verse with each person saying three words. Then have the group say the verse in unison. Finally, have each person recite the verse individually.

Invite everyone to turn to Matthew 5:1-5, using a variety of Bible versions. Ask volunteers to read this passage. Then divide into three groups (a one-person "group" is fine) to study key words. Say something like: *In Bible study, it often helps to examine context to get the meaning of a word.* Distribute copies of the handout sheet with the word study exercise. Group A will be studying "poor in spirit," group B has "mourn," and group C has "meek."

4. APPLY 10 minutes

Direct attention to the handout sheet, "Pilgrim's Progress." Allow 5-8 minutes for completing the graph. Then lead a discussion with the following questions:

- *Of those times when you felt closest to God, how many occurred when you were feeling poor in spirit? Feeling sad? Feeling beaten down or meek?*
- *What did you do during those times when you were feeling poor in spirit (sad, meek, beaten down)? Did anything lead you closer to God?*
- *What did God do in your life during those times?*

Reiterate the positive ways God worked in their lives when they were downcast, based on stories the participants shared. Reassure the participants that it is these conditions, painful as they may be, that invite them *into* the realm of God. This truth is likely counterintuitive; most of us have had experiences with friends or family who distanced themselves from us if we were not happy, or they pressured us to appear happy, even if it was artificial.

Say something like: *When we feel worst, we're often really open to God—sometimes without even knowing it. Jesus says we're blessed, because when we feel most empty, that is when God can fill us.*

5. RESPOND 7 minutes

Return to the "uninviting invitations" from Focus. Ask everyone to think of one other person they know who is feeling poor in spirit, sad, hopeless, or beaten down. After studying these Blessings, what would they invite that person to? Have them complete the invitation, and even give it away if they like.

Close with this benediction straight from the scripture, or a prayer of your own:

> *Blessed are you who are poor in spirit, for yours is the whole realm of heaven!*
> *Blessed are you who mourn, for you shall be comforted!*
> *Blessed are you who are meek, for you shall inherit the earth!*
> *Remember these things in your hearts, and tell others!*

INSIGHTS FROM SCRIPTURE

The Sermon on the Mount is a concise collection of Jesus' instruction to his disciples. This section of Matthew's Gospel is his version of Jesus' teachings. Luke records it with a similar general sequence and structure and content. Some Jesus traditions taught that the Messiah would be an interpreter of Torah (the first five books of the Hebrew scriptures), and even bring a new Torah, or law. Jesus was seen as the fulfillment of that law, and here is a lengthy teaching to inaugurate his messianic authority. It could also have been used by the early Christians as a catechism, teaching the essentials to new believers. This unit will use it the same way.

"Then Jesus took his disciples up onto the mountain and, gathering them around him, he taught them, saying,

'Blessed are the poor in spirit, for theirs is the kingdom of heaven.

'Blessed are the meek; 'Blessed are they that mourn;

'Blessed are the merciful; 'Blessed are they that thirst for justice;

'Blessed are you when persecuted;

'Blessed are you when you suffer;

'Be glad and rejoice, for your reward is great in heaven.'

Then Simon Peter said, 'Are we supposed to know this?'

And Andrew said, 'Do we have to write this down?' And James said, 'Will we have a test on this?'

And Philip said, 'I don't have any paper.'

And Bartholomew said, 'Do we have to turn this in?' And John said, 'The other disciples didn't have to learn this.'

And Matthew said, 'When do we get out of here?' And Judas said, 'What does this have to do with real life?' And Jesus wept."

Author unknown

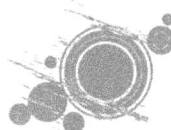

The first set of teachings, the **Blessings** (or the Beatitudes), are pithy—the "Cliff Notes" on how to be a Jesus disciple. As a mini-manual these teachings foretell what we can expect when we commit to Jesus. They aren't so much blessings *upon* as they are insights into the condition of people who do these things or feel these things. They are invitations to live a life according to faith with the help of the Spirit. Though it's not an easy road—rocky, even, at times—the word *blessed* has in it the essence of enjoying a very generous gift from heaven.

There are eight blessings, with extra emphasis on the eighth. In these blessings, Jesus lays out the conditions and characteristics disciples are expected to experience and develop in the course of their discipleship. One way of studying these blessings is to connect them with the major development stages of discipleship: conversion, preparation, and ministry.

Verses 9-12 focus on what to *do* (peacemaking) and *expect* (hardship and persecution) as we live the life and minister as Jesus' disciples. These are not the only ways to minister, but Jesus was being very candid about the conditions of such a life.

›› CONVERSION

While conversion doesn't necessarily *require* poverty of spirit, mourning, and meekness (vv. 3-5), these experiences or qualities are ones that make people especially receptive to a relationship with God, and describe what many Christians experience before and around their conversion.

Right at the start, Jesus pronounces a blessing on "the poor." "The originally bare term stressed the humiliation of poverty," notes Robert H. Gundry in his commentary on Matthew, and refers to "…those whose deprivation led them to cry out for deliverance from oppression," a situation most would view as *hopeless*.

Along with the following two "blessings"—for those who are unutterably sad, and for those who feel beaten down and defeated—we recognize conditions commonly experienced by youth: hopelessness, sadness, and defeat.

Yet following each of these uninviting conditions are rich promises, contrary to what one would expect from the world: "Theirs is the realm of heaven," "They will be comforted," and "They will inherit the earth." Under conditions in which a person is expecting less than zero, Jesus tells us that our God blesses us with comfort, contentment, and nearness to God.

›› PREPARATION AND MINISTRY

Once a person has sunk further than believed possible, it is time to prepare for discipleship (vv. 6-8). The central teachings of Jesus—righteousness, mercy, and spiritual discipline—lead to "purification" of the heart.

As disciples mature in faith, the characteristics necessary for effective ministry continue to develop. Those who once were hopeless begin to realize that with God they have everything they need. Sadness is transformed to empathy for others and even the world. Whereas disciples once were beaten down and crushed, they voluntarily place themselves in a "lowly position" of servitude to God and others. These characteristics help disciples to draw in and minister to others experiencing similar situations.

››› LOOK AHEAD

The next session requires a cake. You'll need a recipe, cake ingredients already measured out, and an already-baked cake if you won't be baking during the session.

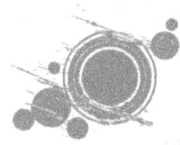

Word Study

Group A:
1. Write down what *you* think "poor in spirit" means (this is an important part of your study!):

2. Look up the following passages that use the same word.*
   - Matthew 11:5
   - Revelation 3:17
   - Mark 10:21
   - 2 Corinthians 8:9
   - Mark 14:7
   - James 2:5

Group B:
1. Write down what *you* think "mourn" means (this is an important part of your study!):

2. Look up the following passages that use the same word.*
   - James 4:9
   - Revelation 18:8
   - Mark 16:10
   - 1 Corinthians 5:2
   - Matthew 9:15

Group C:
1. Write down what *you* think "meek" means (this is an important part of your study!):

2. Look up the following passages that use the same word.*
   - 1 Peter 3:4
   - Matthew 21:5
   - Isaiah 61:1
   - Matthew 11:29
   - Colossians 3:12
   - 2 Corinthians 10:1

> When we feel most empty, that is when God can fill us.

*NOTE: Depending on which translation you have, the word may not always be translated as "poor in spirit," "mourn," or "meek." That's okay. It's the same word in the original Greek.

Salt, Light, and the Good Life : Session 1

Permission is granted to photocopy this handout for use with this session.

Exploring tough questions facing youth today

John Bunyan's classic story, *Pilgrim's Progress*, follows a wayfaring pilgrim named Christian on a journey where he encounters frightful enemies and comforting friends as he seeks to find his true home. Like this wandering pilgrim, we are all on a journey and each of our lives has a particular "look" to it. This graph will create a visual picture of the story of your own journey.

On the left side of the graph is a list of emotions, some of which you have likely experienced. For example, at times in your life you have been at the top of the graph, feeling very content. Maybe at other times you have been at the bottom. And still at others, somewhere in between. Note the timeline that indicates the years of your life. Starting from your earliest significant memories, place a mark above that time to indicate what you were experiencing emotionally.

Move to the next year and do the same. Continue until you reach the present time. Connect the dots. Label high points with an event that reminds you of why you were feeling this way. Label plateaus (flat, horizontal lines) and low points in a similar fashion. If applicable, label the time/period when you started to commit more fully to the life of discipleship.

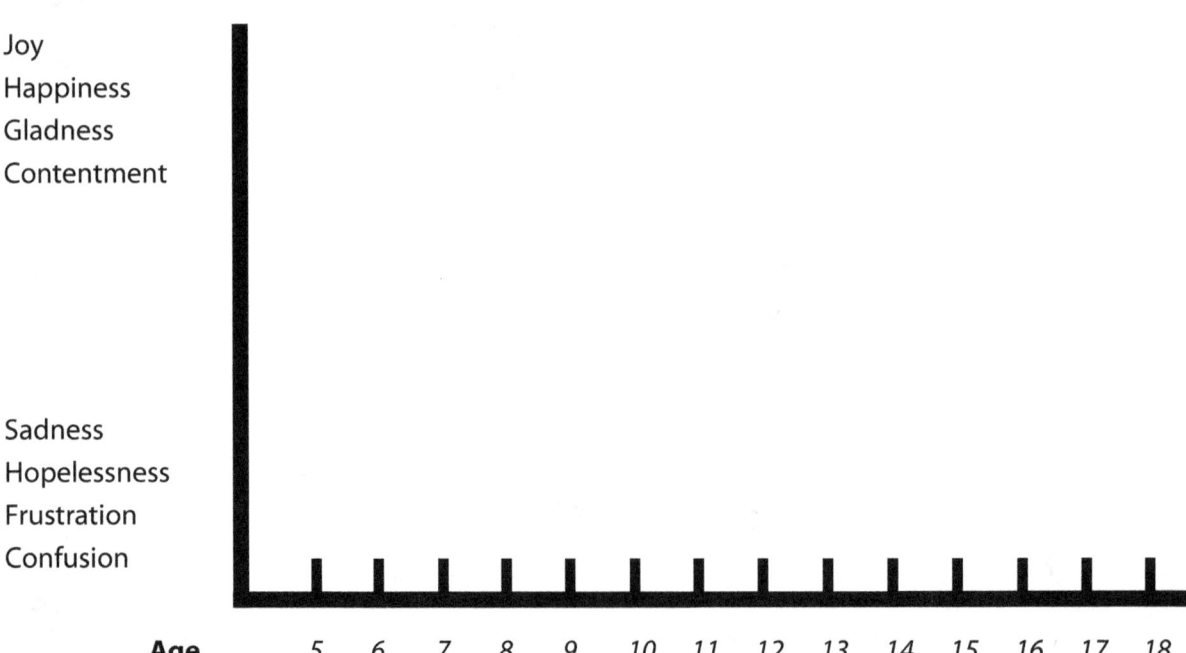

Permission is granted to photocopy this handout for use with this session.

>>> **SESSION 2**

THE BLESSINGS—FOUNDATION/PREPARATION >>>

>> KEY VERSE

"Blessed are those who hunger and thirst for righteousness, for they will be filled." (Matthew 5:6)

>> FAITH STORY

Matthew 5:6-8

>> FAITH FOCUS

The three Blessings—hungering and thirsting for righteousness, being merciful, and being pure in heart—correspond with three fundamental spiritual disciplines that help us grow in knowledge, in heart, and in spirit. Having a strong desire for God's truth; internalizing God's grace, love, and mercy; and keeping one's eyes on God are not only excellent preparations for ministry, but are experiences of faith in and of themselves.

>> SESSION GOAL

Show participants who may be searching for a formula for faith how the *desire* they have is not just something to be fulfilled in the future, but is itself an experience of faith.

>> Materials needed and advance preparation

- Recipe, cake ingredients already measured out (or already-baked cake)
- Index cards (or paper of the same size) and pens/pencils
- Hat or container for distributing papers
- Bibles
- Additional slips of paper prepared with words listed in Apply, *Option A*
- Copies of the handout sheet for Session 2 (Apply, *Option C*)

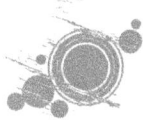 # TEACHING PLAN

1. FOCUS 10 minutes

Baking a Cake. On a table have a recipe and the ingredients for a cake (measure out ahead of time). Ask: *How many of these items are a cake? Is the recipe a cake? How about the set of ingredients?* After briefly exploring these questions, mix the batter, and then bake the cake during the rest of the session, if you can. (If not, have an already-baked cake to share at the end.) Select someone to read the recipe and to guide the other members of the group in combining the ingredients (some members will be needed for cleanup).

In Real Life | Salt, Light, and the Good Life 13

"I ask myself 'Why am I here? Where am I going? What am I working for?' When I imagine my life a successful one I always feel empty. I imagine I'll spend the rest of my life desperately clawing at my goals. When I decide to take a break from my goals, there's nothing but killing time on video games....

I sometimes exercise to feel more fulfilled, but I just think to myself: 'So what if I get even stronger and faster? So what if I get the best-looking clothes and all of the confidence and success I've pursued? So what if I actually finish that story? When I arrive there, it won't mean anything. It'll be just another thing behind me, like everything else.'

I need to find a calling. My thoughts always jump to, 'Climb a mountain. Backpack in China by yourself. Learn a new language. Go skydiving.' These things, however, seem like they've been implanted in my mind by society as the typical 'full life' things. Honestly, I have no idea what I actually want to do. I feel like I'm just working to yearn for the life I've been programmed to desire."

Comment from the Internet

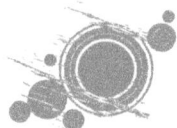

2. CONNECT 5 minutes

Ask the group to figure out which ingredients they might have been able to substitute and still get a cake. For example, the flavoring, the icing, the kind of flour, and the liquid (water vs. milk) are all ingredients that could have been different yet would still produce some kind of cake. Next, ask them which ingredients are really essential. For example, the leavening agent, the flour, and the sweetener are all necessary ingredients for a cake. If you don't have these things, you might be able to cook up something, but it's not likely to be a cake!

3. EXPLORE THE BIBLE 15 minutes

Shift to this activity by saying: *Just as in baking a cake, there are lots of ways to be a disciple of Jesus. But there are also a few essential ingredients to being one, or else you're something else!*

Pass out index cards or small pieces of paper and pens or pencils. Have participants write an anonymous response to the following: *What do you consider one of the most essential ingredients in being a follower of Jesus?*

Put all the cards in a hat or other container and mix them up. Have someone pick one of the cards, read it, and explain why this particular ingredient is important, *even though it is probably not the one they wrote.* Pass the hat to another person and repeat the process. Then have everyone turn to Matthew 5:6-8 to see what ingredients are critical to making a disciple. Invite someone to read this passage.

> **Option:** Memory work. At this point, if you have chosen to have people memorize the Blessings, choose one of the memorization methods mentioned in Session 1 (Explore). Then continue with the questions and discussion below.

Ask: *What are three identifying marks of a disciple according to these Blessings? What similarities are there in the Blessings and the ones we drew? Why are these qualities essential in preparing for discipleship?* (The hunger for truth leads us to search until we find out what is deeply right. We practice mercy because God is merciful. We have the disciplines of prayer, meditation, study, and fasting to help us cleanse our hearts, be open to God, and prepare us for service.)

4. APPLY 10-15 minutes

> **Option A:** Divide into at least two groups for **making commercials**. Hand each group a slip of paper with one of the following items listed: favorite soft drink, best pizza, greatest band, most enticing candy, coolest ride. The task is to create a *craving* in the rest of the group for this item. What happens if you're really hungry for something? What will you do to get it? Have fun presenting your commercials!

Ask: *What kind of persuasion or commercial might you have come up with if your slip of paper said "justice"? Or "righteousness"?* Explain that Jesus is saying that if you're *really* hungry for such a thing, you'll eventually get it, because justice/righteousness is a good thing to be hungry for! And if you're *always* hungry for it, you'll always work to get it.

Go on to **Option A** in Respond, below.

》 Option B: Lead a discussion on whether these three Blessings are related to one another. Is it possible to be righteous and merciful at the same time? Start off with this situation: A ruthless dictator is ousted from his country by revolution. He petitions to return to the country ten years later. In this situation, what does it mean to be hungry for justice? What would it mean to be merciful? What if *you* were that exiled dictator?

Point out that 2 Timothy 2:22 says that "a pure heart seeks righteousness and love," and Philippians 1:10 says that to be pure is to "discern what is best." Being pure doesn't mean being perfect—it means concentrating on God's Way.

Have participants describe a situation from their own lives where they found it difficult or seemingly impossible to show love or mercy. What if someone harmed them or their family, and later came asking forgiveness? Suppose the person never asked forgiveness, but you later were in the position of having to rescue him or her? What's the right thing to do? What's the merciful thing to do? Encourage making up fictional situations if they can't come up with one from their own life.

Invite suggestions for handling the situation(s). It should become evident that youth often feel a conflict between what is right or fair and what is merciful. How do we become people who are merciful *and* righteous?

Go on to **Option A** in Respond, below.

》 Option C: Distribute copies of the handout sheet, "Divine Conversation: The Spiritual Discipline of Prayer," and answer any questions. Then have participants select one of the approaches and spend the rest of the session putting it into practice. Go outside to do the practice, if possible.

Go on to **Option B** in Respond, below.

5. RESPOND 10 minutes

》 Option A: Say something like: *Our appetites and passions for things we love are generally good, if they are directed in a positive way. But any passion requires discipline, even a passion for justice or mercy or for God.*

Hand out index cards and invite participants to write down at least one of their passions. It may be something other people have named for them, or it may be something they know of deep inside, even a passion for God. Beside the passion, have them write a goal for themselves that includes a practical method for disciplining that passion.

Go on to **For both options**, below.

》 Option B: Continue the "Divine Conversation," started in *Option C*, above.

For both options: Close by "breaking the cake" together, using one of these closings: *Go in hunger—for justice, for mercy, for community. You shall find it.* **OR** *God, to those who have hunger, give bread: And to those who have bread, give the hunger for justice* (Latin American prayer).

"Not all who wander are lost."

Bumper sticker

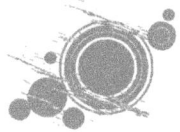

"The shoe that fits one person pinches another; there is no recipe for living that suits all cases."

Carl Jung,
Swiss psychiatrist

"Cursed be the one whose thirst is quenched."

Nikos Kazantzakis,
Greek novelist

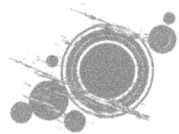

Optional closing: Refer participants to the verse, "Blessed are the pure in heart, for they shall see God," then read this short story.

> There once was a little boy who wanted to meet God. He knew it was a long journey to where God lived, so he packed his suitcase with Twinkies and a six-pack of root beer, and started out.
>
> When he had gone about three blocks, he met an old woman. She was sitting in the park, staring at some pigeons. The boy sat down next to her and opened his suitcase. He was about to take a drink from his root beer when he decided instead to offer her a Twinkie. She gratefully accepted and smiled at him. Her smile was so pretty that the boy wanted to see it again, so he offered her a root beer. Once again, she smiled at him. The boy was delighted.
>
> They sat there all afternoon eating and smiling, yet they never said a word.
>
> As it grew dark, the boy got up to leave. Before he had gone more than a few steps, he turned around, ran back to the old woman, and gave her a hug. She gave him her biggest smile ever. When the boy opened the door to his own home a short time later, his mother commented on the look of joy on his face. "What did you do today that made you so happy?" He replied, "I had lunch with God. You know what? She's got the most beautiful smile I've ever seen!"
>
> Meanwhile, the old woman, also radiant with joy, returned to her home. Her son was stunned by the look of peace on her face. "Mother, what did you do today that made you so happy?" She replied, "I ate Twinkies in the park with God. You know, he's much younger than I expected."

(story told by Pastor David McKellip)

LOOK AHEAD

For the next session, **Option A** in Apply is to have a guest come to be interviewed. This individual should have ministry experience that involved some aspect of peacemaking and reconciliation.

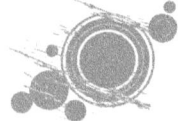

INSIGHTS FROM SCRIPTURE

The Blessings reveal essential ingredients for the making of a disciple of Jesus. By diligently combining essential ingredients, we prepare for a life of service to our Creator. Though other ingredients may also be present, righteousness, compassion/mercy, and spiritual discipline are fundamental preparation for interacting and living as a disciple in the world. These three fundamentals provide disciples with the tools to grow in knowledge, in heart, and in spirit.

Jesus follows each of the three fundamental conditions with powerful promises: (1) "They will be filled" (with righteousness), (2) "They will be shown mercy," and (3) "They will see God." With these promises, Jesus assures his disciples that their pursuit of the fundamentals will be worthwhile. Sometimes the reward is simply the state of *being* hungry, or *being* merciful, or *having* the fervent desire to do what God would want of us. The yearning we have for justice, for mercy, for seeing God, is not just future anticipation, but can be in itself an experience of faith. In these Blessings Jesus is saying that if you're really hungry for such a thing, you'll eventually get it, because justice/righteousness (for example) is a good thing to be hungry for! And if you're always hungry for it, you'll always work to get it.

›› HUNGER FOR RIGHTEOUSNESS, THIRST FOR MERCY

Many people experience these fundamental yearnings shortly after they have converted and are zealous for the Way of Jesus. It is in this state that we "hunger and thirst for righteousness," or *the nature of God's truth* and what it means to be a Christian. In prayer and study, the new disciple starts to realize that *love, grace, and mercy* are central to this truth. Jesus criticized the Pharisees for missing this simple, profound reality.

›› SPIRITUAL DISCIPLINE

Following up on this truth requires regular communion with God, to practice allowing the divine mind and heart to emerge within us. Becoming a complete disciple is the joyous work of a lifetime. The growing disciple begins with personalizing and internalizing righteousness, compassion/mercy, and spiritual discipline, as outlined in these Blessings.

›› FINDING BALANCE

Jesus models the balance of these principles in his interaction, for example, with the Samaritan woman. He (1) approached her with acceptance and compassion, (2) provided her with just enough truth to start her on the road to discipleship (too much truth is usually very hard to take), and (3) then retreated to pray and meditate (spiritual discipline and listening for God's direction).

Other scriptures combine these essentials as well: 2 Timothy 2:22 says that a pure heart seeks righteousness and love. Philippians 1:10 explains that to be pure is to discern what is best. "Purity" may be a turnoff for some youth. Help them understand that being pure doesn't mean being perfect—it means *concentrating on God's Way*.

In her book *Almost Christian: What the Faith of Our Teenagers Is Telling the American Church*, Princeton Theological Seminary professor Kenda Creasy Dean concludes that, "Youth are bored with an American faith tied to the cult of being nice rather than being committed to Jesus." Yet "we're not called to be nice, but to be *holy*, a word that implies justice, kindness, and humility before God."

Jesus preached and lived a balance of righteous zeal with mercy and compassion. Dare we invite youth to radical discipleship rather than bland Christian tourism? These Blessings—these fundamentals of discipleship—can sow the seeds of powerful spiritual discipleship, especially when focused by disciplines of prayer, meditation, study, and fasting as anchors for life and work as a disciple of the Way.

"God, to those who have hunger, give bread: And to those who have bread, give the hunger for justice."

Latin American prayer

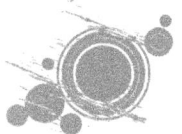

Divine Conversation:
the spiritual discipline of prayer

Just as athletes, musicians, or actors train to learn and master their crafts, good "pray-ers" give conversation with God the same kind of creative energy and discipline.

In Real Life — Exploring tough questions facing youth today

> **PRAYER DEFINITIONS:**
> "Conversing with God, talking and listening."
> "[Prayer] ushers us into perpetual communion with God."
> "To pray is to change."
> "All who have walked with God have viewed prayer as the main business of their lives."
> "Listening for the heartbeat of God."
> "Prayer is learning."
> "Like a child we are to come—openness, honesty, and trust mark the communication of children with their parents."
> (Richard J. Foster, *Celebration of Discipline*)

Here are four different approaches to prayer. Select one and practice it right now.

- Go outside for a walk. In a sheltered place, stop, close your eyes, and notice all the different sounds you can hear. Just notice them; don't think about them. Now open your eyes, and without moving around, do the same with all the different things you can see from where you are. Now notice physical sensations in the same way—the temperature, your clothing, the way your skin tingles, all the smells you are aware of. Just notice these things; don't think about them. Draw a picture of the sensations—sights, sounds, smells that came to you—with yourself in the middle. What does this suggest about your Creator? Your relationship to God? How would you respond to the One who created you in such exquisite detail?

- Take a walk with Jesus. What does he notice? What does he point out to you? What do you notice? Speak of it together. Notice how he clearly delights in you. "Can we do this more often?" he asks. You reply, telling him why you like to be with him, or why it's hard to be with him. When you come back from the walk, follow up with him in the way that makes the most sense to you, just as you might after a first date.

- The word for "breath" in scripture is the same as the word for "spirit" or "wind." This is what the Creator blew into the clay of the first humans—divine Breath. In a quiet place, become aware of how your breath moves into your nose, down your throat, into your lungs, and expands your belly. Focus just on this breath, following it as it moves from your inhalation to your exhalation and then repeats. When thoughts arise, simply return your focus to your breath. Practice paying attention to your breath, repeating the words: "You ride on the wings of the wind" (from Psalm 104).

- Imagine that you are with Jesus in the Garden of Gethsemane. The angels have come and strengthened him for the day to come. Let him tell you what he is thinking, how he feels. Be present to him as much as you can. Listen to his sorrow and his hope.

Salt, Light, and the Good Life : Session 2

Permission is granted to photocopy this handout for use with this session.

Exploring tough questions facing youth today

>>> **SESSION 3**

THE BLESSINGS— COMMISSION/MINISTRY >>>

>> KEY VERSE
"Blessed are the peacemakers, for they will be called children of God." (Matthew 5:9)

>> FAITH STORY
Matthew 5:9-12

>> FAITH FOCUS
These Beatitudes/Blessings focus on peacemaking and the fact that doing the right thing could invite persecution and false charges. However, the rewards—full adoption by God and full access to and use of heavenly resources—are enormous.

>> SESSION GOAL
Urge participants to integrate regular peacemaking and reconciliation into their lives as disciples.

>> Materials needed and advance preparation

- Chalkboard/chalk or newsprint/markers
- Bibles
- Internet connection (option in Explore)
- A guest to be interviewed (Apply, Option A)
- Paper and pens/pencils
- Shovel, sturdy waterproof container, and spot to bury time capsule (Respond, Option A)
- Matches, fireproof container, water (for burning prayers in Respond, Option B)

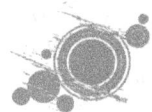

TEACHING PLAN

1. FOCUS 8 minutes

Protection. Tell participants you're going to say a word or a phrase. They are to come up with words or phrases that tell how they are **usually protected** from the thing(s) you mention. Jot their responses on the chalkboard or newsprint. (You'll be eliciting home, school, and community rules designed for community protection.) Words/phrases to use (add some of your own):

- Food poisoning
- Flu
- Being hit by a car
- Contaminated water
- Shoplifters
- Being shot at
- Bicycle accidents
- Skunk bites
- Police brutality
- Environmental poisons

In Real Life | Salt, Light, and the Good Life   19

2. CONNECT 7 minutes

Risk. Now move from *protection* to *risk*. Ask the following questions, each with varying elements of risk. If participants answer yes, they should indicate it by standing. If no, have them remain seated. Give people a few moments to think through the situation before responding. Would you:

- Kiss your dad good-bye in front of the school?
- Hitchhike?
- Give a stranger rescue breaths and CPR?
- Drink from a mountain stream?
- You're coaching soccer when a kid at the field gets hurt. Would you take the child home into a neighborhood you don't know well?
- A smoke detector goes off in a locked trailer, and you think you hear a trapped animal crying. Would you break in?
- Expose a teacher who's being unethical?
- Participate in a political demonstration?
- You are invited to a party attended by many fascinating people you've never met. Would you go if you had to go by yourself?

3. EXPLORE THE BIBLE 15 minutes

Shift to this activity by saying: *Though most of us get the protection we need, risks increase as we start making decisions for ourselves. Being a peacemaking disciple of Jesus may be one of the riskiest decisions of all.*

> **Option: Memory work.** At this point, if you have chosen to have participants memorize the Blessings, choose one of the memorization methods mentioned in Session 1 (Explore). Then continue with the questions and discussion below.

Have someone read Matthew 5:9-12. Comment on these Blessings by noting that the core of ministry is peacemaking. Yet Jesus was very candid about the response to such risky ministry: persecution. Then, invite participants to do an Internet search for true stories of radical, risky peacemaking. **OR**, tell some or all of the following true stories.

- Guatemalans began telling their stories of suffering in the aftermath of 36 years of civil war. Catholic Bishop Juan Gerardi, founder and coordinator of the Human Rights Office of the Archbishopric of Guatemala, presided over the unveiling of a monument to the civil war's victims, a ceremony that gave many Guatemalans reason for hope. He said, "We want to continue the building of a country different from the one we have now. For that reason, we are recovering the memory of our people. This path has been and continues to be full of risks and can only be built by those who have the strength to confront those risks." Two days later Gerardi was brutally murdered as he entered his home.

- When Oscar Romero became Archbishop of San Salvador in 1977, a mere fourteen families controlled 60 percent of arable land in El Salvador, and most peasants were landless. The country was engulfed in a civil war that would last 12 years and claim 75,000 lives, mostly poor peasants from the countryside. The Salvadoran military, with aid from the United States, protected the wealth and privilege of the elite while sowing terror among the people. In this context, Archbishop Romero consistently spoke out on behalf of the poor who were daily being kidnapped, tortured, and killed. On March 23, 1980, he "ordered" the men of the military to stop the repression of fellow Salvadorans, telling them they were not compelled to follow an immoral order. The following day, he was assassinated.

- In 1982, Enten Eller refused to register for the draft because of his religious convictions as a conscientious objector to war. For taking this stand of conscience, Eller was convicted of a felony and sentenced to 18 months of community service.
- From 1983 to 1985, Jennifer Casolo sheltered Central American refugees when it was illegal to do so. Later, in El Salvador, she worked with church and international groups to pressure the military government to stop human rights abuses. Then, as part of a widespread attack on international Christian workers, Casolo was arrested after police discovered weapons buried in the backyard of her rental—evidently planted by people seeking to frame her. After being detained by the military for more than two weeks, Casolo was released and deported from El Salvador.
- In 2014, hundreds of teenage girls were kidnapped from a school in Chibok, Nigeria, by Boko Haram, an extremist Islamic sect violently seeking a "pure" Islamic state. The school focuses on education, health, and wellness, as well as spirituality and faith formation, but Boko Haram targeted all who were not with them in their ideology. Despite the horrific threats, destruction, and killings, Rebecca Dali, a church leader in the area, organized people to continue to take supplies and food to orphans and refugees affected by the violence. She documented the missing so they would be remembered, and interviewed the girls' families and all the returning girls who were able to escape their captors.
- Sister Dorothy Stang was a Sister of Notre Dame de Namur, who served as a missionary in the Amazon rainforest of Brazil. There, she worked to create programs that empowered local farmers to create self-sufficient communities in which they could both support their families and protect the rainforest. Her work was a threat to the loggers, speculators, and other business interests in the region. As a result, after repeated death-threats, she was gunned down on a dirt road near the Boa Esperanca settlement in rural Para. As the gunmen approached, she opened her Bible and began reading from the Beatitudes: "Blessed are those who hunger and thirst for righteousness."

Read Matthew 5:9-12 one more time. Note for the group that Jesus says we are *blessed* if we are persecuted for serving him. Ask: *How could we possibly be blessed when we are being hurt for serving Jesus? What does he mean?*

Sometimes our efforts at peacemaking and reconciliation draw persecution from the government and other powerful interests, as in the stories above; other times it comes from friends who don't like what we're doing, blow us off, or say hurtful things. Sometimes this kind of treatment comes from members of our own family. *How do stories like those we've heard today make you feel?* (Inspired to remain steadfast? Too far out of my experience? Wanting to do anything to avoid that kind of trouble?)

4. APPLY 10 minutes

>> **Option A:** Invite a person, someone youth will connect with, who has had some experience of risk, even persecution, because of his or her efforts to be a peacemaker (refused military service or registration for reasons of conscience, someone who supported war refugees when it was illegal, lost a job because of whistle-blowing, protested war or the weapons industry). Help the group formulate some questions for an interview before the guest arrives. Samples: *Why did you decide to do what you did? What was your goal? How is this goal related to peacemaking? What did you expect this work to be like before you began it? Did you experience any resistance or persecution as a result of this work?*

"No process of peace can ever begin unless an attitude of sincere forgiveness takes root in human hearts. When such forgiveness is lacking, wounds fester, fueling in the younger generation endless resentment, producing a desire for revenge and causing fresh destruction. Offering and accepting forgiveness is the essential condition for making the journey towards authentic and lasting peace."

St. John Paul II
Message for the World Day of Peace 1997.

>> **Option B:** Read one of many stories from *Why Forgive* (formerly titled *Seventy Times Seven*) by J. Christoph Arnold (http://www.plough.com/en/ebooks/w/why-forgive) on forgiveness and reconciliation. It is available as a free e-book. These stories demonstrate the centrality of forgiveness to reconciliation and peacemaking. If you have access, or can download a story, present it to the group. If not, choose from one of the summaries below.

>> ### Story 1

Marietta Jaeger's 7-year-old daughter was kidnapped from their tent during a camping trip in Montana. Though Marietta's initial reaction was one of rage, she says she soon realized that no amount of anger could bring her daughter back. She "wrestled" with God, and finally sensed that forgiving the kidnapper was the only way she would ever be able to cope with her loss.

She prayed for the kidnapper over the weeks and months that followed. A year after her daughter had been abducted, Marietta received a phone call from the kidnapper, and was surprised at her strange but genuine feeling of compassion for the man at the other end of the line. She was able to record their conversation, but it was still months before he was arrested, and she found out that there was a backbone of a small child among the kidnapper's belongings.

State law offered the death penalty, but Marietta requested that her child's killer be given an alternative sentence of life imprisonment with psychiatric counseling. The tormented young man soon committed suicide. Today, Marietta is part of a group that works for reconciliation between murderers and the families of victims.

>> ### Story 2

Gordon Wilson held his daughter's hand as they lay trapped beneath a mountain of rubble. He and Marie had been attending a peaceful memorial service in Enniskillen, Northern Ireland, when a terrorist bomb went off. By the end of the day, Marie and nine other civilians were dead, and 63 had been hospitalized for injuries. But Gordon refused to retaliate, saying that angry words could neither restore his daughter nor bring peace to Belfast. Gordon struggled to live up to his words. He knew that the terrorists who took his daughter's life were anything but remorseful. Even so, he was misunderstood and ridiculed by many because he refused to seek revenge.

Gordon's forgiveness allowed him to come to terms with his daughter's sudden death, and its effects reached far beyond his own person. At least temporarily, his words broke the cycle of killing and revenge; the local Protestant paramilitary leadership felt so convicted by his courage that they did not retaliate.

>> ### Story 3

As a 10-year-old in Miami, Chris Carrier was abducted and assaulted by a former employee of his father's and left to die in the Florida Everglades. Six days later, Chris was found by a local deer hunter. Chris' head was bloody and his eyes black. He had been stabbed with an ice pick and shot through the head. Miraculously, there was no brain damage, nor did he remember being shot. But Chris was now blind in one eye and could not take part in contact sports. He lived in fear because his abductor was still at large.

When he was 13, he underwent a change. He began to see his nightmare as a blessing rather than a curse. He realized he could have died. He also recognized that he could not stay angry forever, and he decided to turn his back on animosity, revenge, and self-pity.

Years later, Chris found out that someone had confessed to abducting him. Chris visited him the following day, finding a 77-year-old blind man ruined by alcoholism and smoking. He had no family and no friends. Chris writes: "Forgiveness is a gift—it is mercy. It is a gift that I have received and also given away. In both cases it has been completely satisfying." Three weeks later, the man died.

###》 Discussion questions:

- *What are some areas of conflict (bitterness, resentment, anger) that you are aware of that could use some peace?* Some typical conflicts are in relationships at home, school, church, work, or between different ethnic groups in your community.
- *What are some ways to bring peace to these conflicts you've mentioned?*
- *How important is forgiveness in the peacemaking process? How do we bring forgiveness into this process?*
- *How would you encourage a person who is harboring a bitter resentment against someone, like Marietta toward her daughter's killer, of the importance of forgiveness?*
- *What are some different relationships in your community where you have worked as a peacemaker?*
- *Has anyone here experienced persecution for being a Christian?*
- *How did that persecution make you feel and how did you respond to it?*
- *How did God meet you during these times of persecution?*
- *What are some ways to be involved in peacemaking in your community?*

》 **Option C:** Have participants compose a message, either on paper or electronically, to someone whom they have hurt and need forgiveness from, or someone who has hurt them and they are having a difficult time forgiving. Have them explain what action hurt them or what it is that they did to hurt the other. Then have them express how they would like to have been treated or to have behaved. If possible have them express forgiveness or an apology in the message. This message could be to themselves, as it is often difficult to forgive ourselves for something we have done. It could be to a friend, a family member, or someone they aren't friends with or don't like. The message, much like a psalm, could even be to God. Inform them that they do not have to send this message. It is for their eyes only, unless of course they feel moved to take the risky step of peacemaking by sending it.

5. RESPOND 5-10 minutes

》 **Option A:** Make a **peacemaker's time capsule**. Have each person compose a message or prayer for continuing peacemaking, either on paper or electronically. It could be directed to any of the people (living or dead) in the stories told during the session (review the names), or to some peacemaker or volunteer service workers from their parish or community. You might connect with Maryknoll Lay Missioners (mklm.org) or other similar organizations for contact information for specific volunteers and send the message via social media, or write a note to people who could use an encouraging word.

In addition, gather all the paper prayers and messages, and seal them in a container suitable for burying or hiding as a time capsule. Affix the present date to the box, and somewhere in the youth room, instructions that the box is to be opened at least every two years to add names of other peacemakers and prayers. This way, messages and stories of peacemaking go on and on. As a group, either bury or select the capsule site, and mark it. You may want to leave it somewhat accessible for the next few weeks, in case participants think of other people they'd like to add.

If anyone in your group is into geocaching, suggest leaving messages of peace whenever someone goes on a next hike or adventure. If you choose not to do a time capsule, offer the messages and prayers during the offering in worship.

"Whenever you take a stand for truth and justice, you are liable to scorn. Often you will be called an impractical idealist or a dangerous radical. Sometimes it might mean going to jail. If such is the case you must honorably grace the jail with your presence. It might even mean physical death. But if physical death is the price that some must pay to free their children from a permanent life of psychological death, then nothing could be more Christian."

Martin Luther King, Jr.

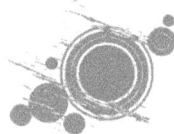

>>> LOOK AHEAD

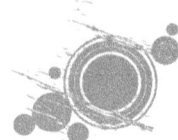

Different materials are needed in Session 4, Focus, depending on which option you choose. For **Option A:** cardboard signs; **Option B:** three flashlights; or **Option C:** an unsalted (bland) food and saltshakers.

>> **Option B:** As part of your response to those currently experiencing persecution for their religious convictions, whatever their religion, conduct a time of silent prayer by having participants write their prayers on a piece of paper. Gather the papers and burn them (in a fireproof container, or outside) as a visible symbol of the suffering being experienced by religious believers throughout the world.

INSIGHTS FROM SCRIPTURE

Work is where people spend a major portion of their time to earn their keep. The third set of Blessings focuses on what disciples can expect as they commit to their work of peacemaking: acceptance of persecution.

>> LIKE PARENT, LIKE CHILD

Most of us can think of ways we are like our parents. It may be a physical aspect, or an attitude or a conviction. Jesus says that people who are working for peace are being like God, their parent. Bringing love, grace, and mercy into a situation (personal, family, neighborhood, war) becomes the primary work and life of the disciples of the Prince of Peace, Jesus Christ.

>> CHILDREN OF GOD

Jesus follows up this recitation of a family tree with some candid observations. He says that faithful actions taken by disciples could invite persecution and hardship. "People will insult you, persecute you, and say all kinds of evil against you because of me."

However, the rewards are enormous: full adoption into God's family as "children of God" as well as access to all the riches of heaven since "[yours] is the realm of heaven" and "great is your reward in heaven." In these final Blessings, the disciples are to weigh costs and rewards. And the reward is a clear sense of what is most important.

Once the disciple starts a work or ministry, there emerge many opportunities for everyday peacemaking: within oneself, in relationship with others, in relationship with God, and within society.

>> PEACE WITHIN...AND WITHOUT

Peacemaking starts with giving *ourselves* love, grace, and mercy. One of the hardest things to do is to speak peace to ourselves regarding shame, guilt, or other things we don't like about ourselves. People who come from dysfunctional families are especially in need of such peace.

Peacemaking in our relationship with others means holding love, grace, and mercy in the relationship. Other words for relational peacemaking include "reconciliation" and "forgiveness."

Coming to humble peace in our relationship with God is the engine that drives all other peacemaking. Disciples who hold rigidly to rules with a narrow view of rights and wrongs need to experience the God of love, grace, and mercy. If they do not, how can they model it for others?

Peacemaking within society involves bringing God's redeeming love, grace, and mercy into worldly situations such as war, racism, broken marriage relationships, and gang violence.

>>> **SESSION 4**

SALT AND LIGHT >>>

>>> KEY VERSE

"You are the light of the world. A city built on a hill cannot be hid." (Matthew 5:14)

>>> FAITH STORY

Matthew 5:13-16

>>> FAITH FOCUS

Jesus says that disciples are to be the ingredient (salt) that gives life flavor. But like all flavoring, it isn't worth much if it can't be tasted. If the disciples lose their "saltiness," they are of little use. He encourages them to be prominent and active with their witnessing and ministry, so that people will notice God's activity in their midst.

>>> SESSION GOAL

Help participants who wonder about their purpose in life see that their principal job is, through their "saltiness" and light, to let God's light in them shine.

>>> **Materials needed and advance preparation**

- Cardboard signs (see Focus, *Option A*, for how to prepare them)
- Three flashlights (Focus, *Option B* and *Option C*)
- Bowls of unsalted (bland) food (peanuts, crackers, popcorn) and saltshakers (Focus, *Option D*)
- Bibles
- Samples of common household herbs and spices for participants to taste (Apply, *Option A*)
- Copies of the handout sheets for Session 4
- Pens/pencils

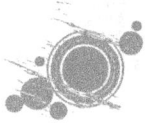

TEACHING PLAN

1. **FOCUS** 6 minutes

>>> **Option A:** Prepare three cardboard signs, each with a different command:
- Stand on one foot.
- Pull your ears.
- Place palms together.

Use black markers on two of the signs and a highlighter (hard to see) on the third. Hang one of the black marker signs where everyone can see it. Put the other under a coat or blanket. Place the "highlighter" sign in a visible place.

Once the group is in the room, tell them that they will play **Simon Says** with you as the leader. Start with a few verbal commands (touch toes, shake a leg, flap arms, etc.). Then simply point to the command on the sign with visible black marking. Then point to the "highlighter" sign. Finally, point to the place where you've hidden the third sign. That should halt the game.

Go on to **Option A** in Connect.

》 Option B: Darken the meeting room, or go to another dark room. Offer three people flashlights. One will have batteries and work fine, one has batteries but is wrapped in a coat or blanket (don't unwrap it), and one has no batteries at all.

Then, play **Mirror**, in which the group must mirror the actions of a leader (no words). Ask the people with flashlights to spotlight the action. Of course, only one flashlight will provide light. Someone will probably complain that the game is stupid (which it is, without sufficient light). Point made.

Go on to **Option B** in Connect.

》 Option C: If you meet in the evening, play flashlight tag outside for 10 minutes or so. Then take away the flashlight and play for another 5 minutes.

Go on to **Option B** in Connect.

》 Option D: Have a few bowls of unsalted food available as a snack (popcorn, crackers, chips). After everybody has had a couple handfuls, set a few saltshakers on the table or floor. How many people salt their portions?

Go on to **Option C** in Connect.

2. CONNECT 2-3 minutes

》 Option A: Ask the group which of the three cardboard signs was most helpful. Why? Why were the others not helpful?

》 Option B: Turn on lights, and ask the group which of the three flashlights was most helpful. Easy answer. (If you played flashlight tag, ask if it made sense to play flashlight tag without a flashlight.) Then ask the group to think about gifts they have that they don't let shine. Talk about what it means to "use it or lose it."

》 Option C: Ask anyone who salted their snacks why they did so. What is the salt doing? It's enhancing, or bringing to life, the flavor of the food.

3. EXPLORE THE BIBLE 10 minutes.

Shift to this activity by saying: *Salt, flavoring, or light doesn't count for much if it's not used. It's a simple concept, but hard to live by.*

> **》 Option: Memory work.** At this point, if you have chosen to have participants memorize portions of Jesus' Sermon, choose one of the memorization methods mentioned in Session 1 (Explore). Then continue with the questions and discussion below.

Have a person read Matthew 5:13 and ask the group: *What does it mean to be the salt of the earth?* Ask them if they know what the phrase "an old salt" means, and remind them of the meaning. How about the phrase, "She's the salt of the earth"? *How does one lose saltiness?* Have another participant read verses 14-16 and then ask: *What do you think Jesus meant about being a light?*

4. APPLY 15 minutes

>> **Option A:** Though Jesus' listeners knew the value of the scarce commodity of salt, this metaphor may sound strange to us today. Try substituting another seasoning! As a group, make a list of common household herbs and spices. To make the application even more pungent, have some of these herbs and spices on hand for participants to smell or taste. Help each other think about what it would mean to be "hot pepper" in the world. Or "baking powder" (leavening). Or "hot cinnamon candies."

>> **Option B:** Say something like: *Christians over the centuries have used spiritual disciplines like prayer, fasting, meditation, and study to stay "salty." In addition, Christians have ministered and brought God's words to the world, thus being light to the world.* Distribute copies of the first handout sheet, "Accepting God's Embrace: Exploring the Ancient Christian Practice of Meditation," which presents the time-honored discipline of meditation with scripture. Spend the remainder of the time having the participants try *lectio divina* with Matthew 5:13-16, or one of the passages listed.

Close with the prayer in Respond, below.

5. RESPOND 7 minutes

>> **Option A:** Pick up one of the flashlights again, and remark to the group that "going apart" is a good way for some people to recharge their batteries. Ask: *How do you recharge your batteries? What would it be like to invite God along when you recharge?*

Conclude with the prayer in **For both options**, below.

>> **Option B:** Help the group brainstorm ways to be salt and light in their parish or community. Here are some ideas for getting started:

- Contrive a "spiritual buddy system" with each other, with regular times for checking in and praying together (or at least sharing prayer concerns).
- Be a peer mentor **OR** mentor younger children. Mentors typically make contact at least once a week to offer encouragement, answer questions, nurture spiritual growth, and affirm the friendship. They should model the faithful life so that the person they mentor will be able to see in them the characteristics of a mature disciple.

If, in their quest to be salt and light, your youth want to branch out to people (peers or younger children) they don't know well, get them started with an exercise in activating asking skills. Pass out copies of the second handout sheet, "Clean Up Your Acts…Asks," and pens/pencils. Have them rephrase the closed-ended questions at the bottom of the handout.

>> **For both options:** Close with this prayer, or one of your own:

Loving God,
  grow in us the spice of life.
Let us be salt, pepper,
  so that those we meet will come to savor You.
God of light and dark,
  shine out from us so bright
  that those we meet
  may be able to read You in our light. AMEN
    (prayer by Lani Wright)

Song option: Sing "You Are Salt for the Earth," by Marty Haugen, a rousing rendition of this scripture passage.

"A farmer is helpless to grow grain; all he can do is to provide the right conditions for the growing of grain. He puts the seed in the ground where the natural forces take over and up comes the grain. That is the way with the spiritual disciplines— they are a way of sowing to the Spirit. The disciplines are God's way of getting us into the ground; they put us where [God] can work within us and transform us."

Richard Foster,
Celebration of Discipline

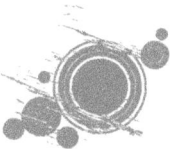

LOOK AHEAD

For the next session you will need a roll of masking tape.

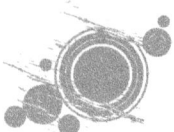

INSIGHTS FROM SCRIPTURE

Using salt and light as metaphors, Jesus defines human purpose. In Jesus' time, salt was used in small quantities as fertilizer to give life to the earth. It was a preservative. It was also critical to have salt in a diet in a hot climate, to replace that lost by the body as it cooled itself through perspiring. Such an important compound also became a medium of exchange.

But Jesus also cautions his disciples. If they "lose their saltiness" they are "no longer good for anything, except to be thrown out and trampled under foot." The reference to "lose their saltiness" is probably related to a practice of some merchants who cheated their customers by diluting the pure salt with gypsum to increase their profits. This practice either reduced the benefits of the salt or made the salt useless.

You've heard the phrases "an old salt," or a "salty character." It usually refers to people who have presence, people you can't miss. You may not always agree with them, but they are true to themselves. They are "characters"—usually respected, rarely ignored. Or how about people who "just light up a room." They're also hard to ignore.

But while salty characters and en-*lightened* people can usually have a worthwhile effect, it's a *community* of salt and light that Jesus highlights in these verses. The Greek word for "you" in this passage is plural, a group of believers. Churches that are dull and tasteless rarely have much effect on their environment; likewise, a church whose lights are out is not visible and effective. This is not a call to boasting and preening in public. Being salt and light is not a question of status, but of *function*—calling forth the zestiness of Life and reflecting the Light the enlightens everyone.

The community of believers is made saltier and brighter whenever one of its members enhances those gifts in him- or herself. Over the years, Christians have used spiritual disciplines like prayer, meditation, study, and fasting to regularly refresh themselves, to keep their "saltiness" strong, that is, to make them more effective disciples.

❯❯ REFLECT THE LIGHT

Jesus follows the metaphor about being salt with one about light. As Jesus was the Light, he expects his disciples to reflect that light to the world. Consider the teaching about the eye being the lamp of the body (Matt. 6:22-23). In first-century Jewish concept, the eye functioned like a house window from which shone whatever was *within* the body. There was as yet no concept of an organ that receives light and images and interprets them in the brain. Thus, if we are still in plural mode, the body of believers is like the window, or lamp, through which the Light of Life shines.

In Luke's version of this teaching, he adds, "those who come in," implying that Jesus expects his disci-ples to be the light for newcomers and to lead them to him. But, like salt that has been diluted, light is useless if it cannot be seen. The purpose of the light is to reflect God and bring all of us closer to God.

Many youth are already active in visible witnessing and ministry such as camps and service projects, being "light" and allowing that of God to shine in them. They may also welcome an introduction to spiritual disciplines as a way to enhance their "saltiness," especially as a way to pause meaningfully in a fast-paced society.

In these few pungent verses, Jesus lays out his expectations of his disciples: We are to share the grace and love we receive from God; we must nurture that which gives us life; and we are to actively share the light that is given to us, so that others experience the love of God. For youth who are looking for a purpose in life, this passage is clear: Their principal job is, through their "saltiness" and light, to let God's light in them shine.

ACCEPTING GOD'S EMBRACE: Exploring the Ancient Christian Practice of Meditation

In Real Life
Exploring tough questions facing youth today

A very ancient art of listening for God's voice is known as *lectio divina*. *Lectio* means "to read" or "to listen". The art of *lectio divina* begins with cultivating the ability to listen deeply. Just as the prophet Elijah listened for the still, small voice of God, we, too, can learn to listen for God—a discipline that can help keep us flavorful and full of light.

In order to hear someone speaking softly, we must learn to be silent. It is impossible to hear gentle sounds if we are constantly speaking or are surrounded with noise. The first step of *lectio divina*, therefore, requires that we quiet down in order to hear God. Find a quiet place where external distractions can be minimized. In order to become silent on the inside, some Christians focus on their breathing; others gently recite a "prayer phrase" (like "Lord Jesus, have mercy on me" or "Come to me"). Use whatever helps you, and allow yourself to enjoy the silence for a few moments.

STEP 1: *Lectio*. The reading and listening of *lectio divina* is very different from the way we typically read magazines, books, and even the Bible. Read slowly. Combine this slow reading with a reverential listening for the still, small voice of God that will speak not loudly, but intimately.

STEP 2: *Meditatio*, or simply, meditation. This step begins when we have found a passage in scripture that speaks to us in a personal way. We "chew" on it. This can be done by gently repeating the passage 5, 10, or 20 times (there really is no limit) and emphasizing different parts of it when it is read. You can personalize it by inserting your own name into the passage at appropriate places.

While softly, slowly repeating the verses, we simultaneously ask and listen for God to speak from this passage. Do not be afraid of internal distractions; memories or thoughts are simply parts of yourself that you can give to God along with the rest of your self. Listen for gentle words of encouragement or correction and an invitation to enter more deeply into God's presence.

STEP 3: *Oratio*, or prayer. Prayer is simply loving conversation with the One who has invited us into a divine embrace. It can also involve offering to God parts of ourselves that we have previously believed unacceptable. God invites us to hold up our most difficult and pain-filled experiences and gently recite over them the word or phrase given to us in the meditation.

STEP 4: *Contemplatio*, or contemplation. It means simply resting in the presence of the One who has invited us to accept the transforming embrace. Be silent, let go of your own words; simply enjoy the experience of being in the presence of Someone who loves you.

This process of *lectio divina* won't be mastered in a day. You may not feel comfortable doing it the first few times. There will be times when you don't feel as if God has spoken to you. Don't give up! Many have found this form of meditation with scripture to be the greatest source of intimacy in their relationship with God. The Bible truly becomes a source of nourishment that will sustain you for a period of time. Also, when practiced on a regular basis, it is good to give yourself a minimum of about 30 minutes to work through this process. Because of its length, you may want to do it only once or twice a week.

Suggested passages (either in whole or in part): Matthew 11:28-30; Mark 10:43-45; Luke 5:31-32; John 10:14-15; Romans 5:6-11; Romans 8:31-39; Galatians 2:20-21; Ephesians 1:3-8*a*; Ephesians 2:1-10; Ephesians 4:32; Philippians 1:6; Philippians 2:1-11; Colossians 2:13-14; 1 Peter 5:6-7; 1 John 4:7-11; and 1 John 4:18-19.

(Source: condensed and modified version of a paper by Fr. Luke Dysinger, O.S.B., entitled "Accepting the Embrace of God: The Ancient Art of Lectio Divina.")

Salt, Light, and the Good Life : Session 4

Permission is granted to photocopy this handout for use with this session.

Clean Up Your ~~Acts~~... Asks
Tips for Peer Mentoring

In Real Life
Exploring tough questions facing youth today

Sometimes starting out a mentoring relationship can seem awkward. Beyond chit-chat about daily activities, how do you dig into things that really matter, without turning somebody off? Answer: Ask the right questions. The questions we ask can either open up communication or close it down. This calls for three important skills:

1. **BE SENSITIVE.** If we ask questions that show insensitivity to the problems and feelings of our friends, it sabotages the natural flow of communication. For example, a male student started asking a bunch of questions about suicide. A female student sitting beside him had just lost a boyfriend to suicide. He ignored her tears and kept asking his questions. Don't ask questions for which others are not ready.

2. **ASK OPEN-ENDED QUESTIONS.** These encourage people to talk more about themselves, a problem, or a belief. Open-ended questions: How do you get along with your sister? How are you feeling about the amount of English homework lately? (Closed-ended: How many siblings do you have? Did you finish your homework?) There's nothing wrong with closed-ended questions most of the time, but developing the skill of asking open-ended questions means thinking through questions carefully before asking them, so that they draw out more than one- or two-word answers.

3. **ASK QUESTIONS THAT TAKE CONVERSATION TO DEEPER LEVELS.** Don't force a conversation. Invite it. If your friend seems unwilling or uninterested, back off. For example, a friend likes a kind of music you can't stand. Instead of saying, "Why do you listen to junk like that?" ask "I notice you really like (type of music). I've never been into it much. Why do you suppose people have such different tastes in music?" **OR** "What is it about music that really turns us on?" Such an approach acknowledges that we may have a difference of opinion, but it seeks to develop understanding and probes deeper concerns.

To practice, try rephrasing these closed-ended questions. Remember, closed-ended questions can be answered in one or two words. Open-ended questions invite sharing.

CLOSED-ENDED QUESTIONS	OPEN-ENDED QUESTIONS
Do you have a big family?	What's your family like?
Are you going to college?	
Do you plan to get married?	
Where are you working now?	
Didn't you think that movie was good?	
Did you pass the math test?	
Do you argue a lot with your parents?	
Are you "born again"?	

(From "Activating Asking Skills" adapted from *Peer Evangelism: Youth and the Big, Scary "E" Word*.)

Permission is granted to photocopy this handout for use with this session.

Exploring tough questions facing youth today

>>> **SESSION 5**

JESUS AND THE LAW >>>

>>> KEY VERSE

"Do not think that I come to abolish the law or the prophets; I have come not to abolish but to fulfill." (Matthew 5:17)

>>> FAITH STORY

Matthew 5:17-48

>>> FAITH FOCUS

Contrary to some rumors about his teaching, Jesus emphasized that his aim was not to challenge the laws given by God to Moses, but to fulfill them. He meant to recover them for their original intent—that biblical laws be rooted in love. He demonstrated that it is not simply what we do or say in worship, but what we do in our daily life that determines how well we are abiding by these laws.

>>> SESSION GOAL

Help participants who have a strong sense of justice avoid legalism by seeing that Jesus returned biblical laws to their roots: Love.

>>> Materials needed and advance preparation

- Mark a large triangle on the floor or ground (see Focus)
- Bibles
- Paper and pencils/pens
- Roll of masking tape
- Index cards (Apply, Option B)

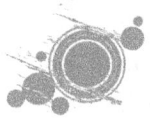

TEACHING PLAN

1. FOCUS 6-8 minutes

Ask participants to place themselves at any of three points on a triangle, according to their reactions to the following set of rules. Designate one point of the triangle as "Don't do it in front of a leader." Another point of the triangle is "Don't even think about it, period." The third point of the triangle is "It's a stupid rule." They must choose one of the triangle points and stand there. Take note of where people stand. Ask: *What do you think these school rules mean?*

1. No guns or knives.
2. No swearing.
3. No firecrackers.
4. No alcohol or other drugs.
5. No cigarettes.
6. No leaving campus during school hours.

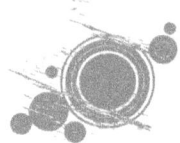

"There is no need for either God or [hu-]man to punish evildoers but that their lives are sufficient, all distraught and ruined as they are by their own villainy."

Plutarch, quoted in *Eleni*, by Nicholas Gage

LOOK AHEAD

The next session calls for a few books of hairstyles from a hair salon (**Option A** in Focus). Another option asks for an array of hairbrushes, bows, barrettes, and ties. Yet another option asks for a page of "personal ads" (from a newspaper or from online sources).

2. CONNECT 7 minutes

Pick one of the rules toward which most people responded either very much alike or very differently, and invite participants to explain why they responded the way they did. How does the enforcement of the "no swearing" rule (or any of the other ones on the list) make them feel? Ask if they understood the intent of each of the rules (especially zero in on any that participants thought were "stupid" rules). Why do they think the rules were created? Do they have people's best interests in mind, or do they benefit only a few?

3. EXPLORE THE BIBLE 15 minutes

Shift to this activity by saying: *When some people look at the Bible, all they see is a bunch of laws or rules. But Jesus wanted people to see that at the heart of it all, there has to be, well, a <u>heart</u>.*

Select a volunteer from the group to read Matthew 5:17. To explore Matthew 5:17-48 (a very big chunk of writing) divide the group into smaller groups, and offer several options for tackling this part of the Sermon. Adapt your approach to the needs of your group:

1. Have one group read the sections on anger, adultery, and oaths, and have a second group read the sections on divorce, retaliation, and love for enemies (for the logic behind this division see Insights, below).
2. Assign only one heading (murder, divorce, etc.) per group.

Pass out paper and pencils/pens. Have participants identify and examine three things:

- What is the *original law* and its literal meaning?
- What is the *intent* of the law according to Jesus?
- What approach to the law is Jesus condemning? Affirming? (If you need to, point out that it is possible to fulfill the letter of the law without fulfilling its intent.) Consider if it is possible to fulfill the intent without also fulfilling the literal meaning.

Tell them to look for the formulaic clue, "You have heard it said,... but I say to you...." Ask them to be ready to give a brief report on their findings to the group. When the time is up gather the group and have them share.

4. APPLY 10 minutes

>> **Option A:** Instruct the group to form a line, shoulder to shoulder, with each person facing in the same direction. Inform them that they are going to be asked a series of yes or no questions. If they answer no to a question, have them take *one step forward*. If they answer yes, they *step back*. **No = Forward; Yes = Back.**

Before you begin, have them mark where they started on the floor with a piece of masking tape. Possible questions to ask (add some of your own, but make sure that they will elicit a clear-cut yes or no):

- *Have you murdered anyone?* They all step forward.
- *Have any of you ever been angry or felt resentment toward someone?* Most should step back.
- *Do you show hatred to people you meet, to your neighbor?* Most participants will answer no and take a step forward.
- *Have you ever spoken negatively about someone behind his or her back?* Most will likely answer yes and take a step back.
- *Have you ever told a lie and someone got hurt for it?*
- *Have you ever found a way to lie without really lying, like leaving out what really happened?*

Draw out the point that it is often easy to follow the literal meaning of the law without following the heart of it. And that by fulfilling the literal meaning alone we don't make much progress spiritually. We end up finishing pretty close to where we started out (as evidenced by where they stand in relation to their taped starting points).

》》 **Option B: Legal eagles.** Divide into two groups of lawyers to discuss the *letter of the law* (or custom), and the *heart* of it (or the intent) in each of the cases below. Use index cards, as needed.

For each of the infractions listed below (or as many as you want to tackle), one group of lawyers will argue to enforce the law or custom. They must explain the dangers, social and ecological, of not sticking with the law. With each new case, switch which group argues the letter of the law/custom.

After they present their case, the other group of lawyers will explain what they believe should be the *spirit* of the law/custom in the case. What solutions may be possible?

Note: Be careful! In some cases the infraction follows the letter of the law, but not the spirit, and in others, the infraction may follow the spirit, but not the letter. Also, if you have a large group, have two people act as co-judges in the cases.

- **Law/custom:** No hunting on public lands. **Infraction:** Aboriginal people hunt there anyway as part of a sacred ceremony.
- **Law/custom:** No gambling in the province/state. **Infraction:** Riverboat gambling accepted (because it's on water, not land).
- **Law/custom:** To play on the church softball team one must attend church at least half the Sundays in a month during the playing season. **Infraction:** Some players show up only for a half-hour of worship two of the four Sundays in June and July, and on Christmas and Easter.
- **Law/custom:** Steer clear of people who get into trouble with the law. **Infraction:** Make friends with someone who's been in trouble with the law.
- **Law/custom:** It's illegal to harbor an illegal immigrant. **Infraction:** Someone is in your country illegally, and wants asylum in your church. If they return to their own country they will likely be tortured or killed.

5. RESPOND 7 minutes

Help participants rewrite Jesus' laws (concerning anger, adultery, divorce, oaths, retaliation, and enemies) so the *intent* is clear to everyone in the group.

Conclude with a prayer for courage to be honest with ourselves when we are simply following the letter of the law but not the intent. Ask God to create in us clean hearts, and to renew a right spirit within us.

》》
"Every [human] lives in two realms, the internal and the external. The internal is that realm of spiritual ends expressed in art, literature, morals and religion. The external is that complex of devices, techniques, mechanisms and instrumentalities by means of which we live. Our problem today is that we have allowed the internal to become lost in the external. We have allowed the means by which we live to outdistance the ends for which we live…. This does not mean that we must turn back the clock of scientific progress…. But our moral and spiritual 'lag' must be redeemed. When scientific power outruns moral power, we end up with guided missiles and misguided [humans]. Our hope for creative living in this world house that we have inherited lies in our ability to re-establish the moral ends of our lives in personal character and social justice. Without this spiritual and moral reawakening we shall destroy ourselves in the misuse of our own instruments."

Martin Luther King, Jr.,
"The World House"

> "[T]he true defenders of doctrine are not those who uphold its letter, but its spirit; not ideas but people; not formulae but the gratuitousness of God's love and forgiveness. This is in no way to detract from the importance of formulae, laws and divine commandments, but rather to exalt the greatness of the true God, who does not treat us according to our merits or even according to our works but solely according to the boundless generosity of his Mercy."
>
> Pope Francis

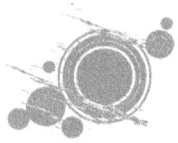

INSIGHTS FROM SCRIPTURE

Contrary to some rumors about his teaching, Jesus emphasized that his aim was not to challenge the laws given by God to Moses, but to fulfill them, to return them to the original intent of sustaining community life for all. Many Jews believed that in the messianic age misunderstandings about God's laws, Torah, would be cleared up. Torah (the law given by God to Moses), was the glue that held Jews together in exile and in wandering. Even though there was a great variety of belief systems among first-century Jews, the memories of God's action in the past fueled their anticipation of the ideal future of God's reign. Who would usher in this future? It would be someone who would correspond to an ideal figure of the past: Moses.

RETURN TO THE ROOT

Matthew was sensitive to his Jewish hearers, but at the same time he was compelled to present Jesus as a new and even greater Moses, the One who brings God's new covenant. Jesus proclaimed, "Do not think that I have come to abolish the law or the prophets; I have come not to abolish but to fulfill." He surely incurred wrath of the religious authorities with his jab and warning, "Unless your righteousness exceeds that of the scribes and Pharisees, you will never enter the kingdom of heaven." Jesus returned biblical laws to the root: Love.

YOU HAVE HEARD IT SAID...

During Jesus' time, murder, adultery, and breaking an oath were three of the worst crimes a person could commit against another human being. Beyond the prohibition against violently taking another person's life, Jesus also condemned the festering anger that led to such violence, including abusive language that escalates ill will.

Adultery also abused relationships by stealing another man's wife (who was considered her husband's property). The penalty for adultery was death by stoning. Again, Jesus takes the rule further, knowing that it is the thought that begins the deed. The problem is not that a man looks at a woman, but that he looks at her "for the purpose of lusting after her" (trans. by Hale, in *Matthew*, Interpretation series). As for divorce, it was possible in Jesus' day for a discontented man simply to declare divorce when he felt like it (though usually on charges of adultery), and put a woman out of the house with minimal economic prospects available to her.

...BUT I SAY TO YOU...

The next three verses, concerning oaths, retaliation, and love for enemies, involved acts that in Jesus' time appeared righteous, but *could* harm another human. Oaths were very common during Jesus' time. However, sophisticated people attached conditions to their oaths. This action could, in effect, nullify any agreement one person might have with another. The passage also speaks against the reckless use of oaths, in which there is no real intention to follow through. If truth is already in the words, there is no need to supply an oath on top of that.

Originally, the ancient (pre-biblical) compensatory code of an "eye for an eye"—the *lex talionis*, or "law of retaliation"—*restricted* retaliation by requiring that it be equitable, neither excessively harsh nor excessively lenient. Few biblical laws are repeated three times; this is one of those few (in Exodus, Deuteronomy, Leviticus). In the Talmud, the fundamental

Jewish legal text, multiple rabbis conclude that the phrase means nothing other than financial compensation, the *value* of an eye for an eye, and in Judaism the literal reading eventually became heretical, notes Yale scholar Joel S. Baden (see http://religion.blogs.cnn.com/2014/07/08/eye-for-an-eye-the-bibles-role-in-revenge-attacks/). Revenge is only to be arbitrated by a third party (of community elders, of civil authorities) who settle the price of monetary compensation, declare the terms of retaliation, and put a stop to the cycle of blood vengeance.

Knowing the hearts of the Pharisees, who had made a divine principle for the courts into a matter of daily vendettas, Jesus instead returned to the spirit of the Hebrew law: We are not to seek retribution, not to demand recompense for wrongs done to us.

>> HOW ON EARTH...?

The admonition to love enemies had to be the toughest of all. But Douglas Hale has pointed out that the verbs love and hate in this passage are not so much about *feelings* as they are about positive or negative *actions*. Jesus calls us to let go of hateful actions, even to someone hostile. Letting go of that which only escalates tension, while coming from an unexpected angle of positive action, will at least keep you from sinking to the same depths as your tormentor.

Jesus taught that as his followers we are to ignore personal insults, which is the meaning of turning the other cheek. Christians are to give more of material goods, time, or labor than demanded of us, even if the demands are wrongful; to loan to those who want to borrow; to love our enemies; and to pray for those who persecute us.

>>> **SESSION 6**

HEAVENLY TEACHINGS— DO THE RIGHT THING >>>

>>> KEY VERSE

"Beware of practicing your piety before others in order to be seen by them; for then you have no reward from your Father in heaven." (Matthew 6:1)

>>> FAITH STORY

Matthew 6:1–7:29

>>> FAITH FOCUS

Jesus says religious practices such as giving to the poor, praying, and fasting are for God, not for public recognition. In a series of rigorous ethical teachings, he also puts money and worry in their places. He concludes by providing pointers on how to stay on course on the rocky, but ultimately satisfying, road with God.

>>> SESSION GOAL

Show youth, who constantly seek approval, that doing the right thing is not so much about how people see us but how God sees us.

>>> Materials needed and advance preparation

- Books of hairstyles from a hair salon, or images found online (Focus, *Option A*)
- An array of hairbrushes, bows, barrettes, and ties (Focus, *Option B*)
- Page of "personal ads" from a newspaper or online, with a legend of abbreviations used (Focus, *Option C*)
- Paper and pens/pencils
- Bibles
- Small slips of paper, basket or hat (Explore, *Option B*)

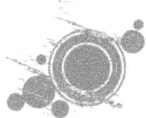

TEACHING PLAN

1. FOCUS 5 minutes

Humans tend to judge based on externals; we'll see later how God looks on *intent* instead.

>>> **Option A:** Using photos depicting various hairstyles, ask participants to say, in just a few words, *what the person might be trying to say with their hairstyle.* Examples: What motivates someone to dye their hair? To dread? To shave it off?

In Real Life | Salt, Light, and the Good Life   39

> **Option B:** Provide an array of hairbrushes, bows, barrettes, and ties, and ask for a few volunteers (guys or girls) to be **hairstyle models**. Have other participants experiment on the person to come up with at least three hairstyles that each say something different about the same person.

> **Option C:** Direct attention to a page (newspaper or online) of "personals." Have each person compose a **personal ad** or create a **Facebook profile** or **Tweet** an introduction, and get readers to want to meet them. Pass out paper and pencils/pens, if needed.

2. CONNECT 7 minutes

Lead a brief discussion about being judged based on one's external appearance. Ask if they've ever experienced being judged only by what they wear or how they look. If the group worked up personal ads, ask how it would feel to be judged solely on what they could fit into a few lines in a personal ad. Did anybody embellish their description to attract someone?

3. EXPLORE THE BIBLE 20 minutes

Shift to this activity: *As much as we may want to look good to others, Jesus said that living rightly is not so much about how others see us but about how God sees us.*

> **Option A:** Break into three groups. Each group will read one of three selections from the Sermon on the Mount (6:1-18, 6:19–7:12, and 7:13-29). Then identify, compose, and compare God's perspective and the world's perspective for each teaching in their selection (such as giving to the poor, prayer, and fasting for 6:1-18). Have each group share their findings.

> **Option B:** In order to cover this large section of the Sermon, play a version of **Charades**. Write the passage locations on small slips of paper (see list below; copy locations, including the summaries). In teams (two or more, depending on the size of your group), have someone from each team pick a slip of paper and act out the charade clues, *without* using the passage location. Use Bibles to connect the clues. The team that comes up with the correct summary first wins that round. Then have another person choose another slip of paper, and so on.

- Matt. 6:1-4 (giving to the poor)
- Matt. 6:16-18 (fasting)
- Matt. 6:19-21 (heart lies with your treasure)
- Matt. 6:22-23 (healthy eye)
- Matt. 6:24-34 (worry about tomorrow/money)
- Matt. 7:1-5 (judging others)
- Matt. 7:7-11 (ask, search, knock)
- Matt. 7:12 (golden rule)
- Matt. 7:13-14 (narrow gate/hard road)
- Matt. 7:15-20 (tree and its fruit)

4. APPLY 15 minutes

Either divide up the areas of Jesus' teaching listed above in Explore, or work as a group: Rewrite each teaching (just one or two sentences) as *actions* that would please God. For example, Matt. 6:16-18, could be, "When you're fasting, don't complain about being hungry. Don't boast about how your fast is going."

> "Some people think God solves all your problems. But my belief in God creates problems. When you know the difference between right and wrong, you have to take responsibility for your acts and deal with the effect of your wrongdoing."

David Eugene Edwards, singer

> "Live every day so you wouldn't be afraid to sell your parrot to the town gossip."

Will Rogers, 20th-century humorist

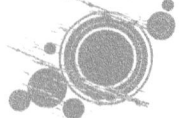

5. RESPOND 10 minutes

Say: *During times of persecution, the early Christians used the symbol of the fish to identify themselves to one another. It could be done on the sly, scraping the outline of a fish in the dust, so that only someone who knew the symbol would respond to it. It was identification, but also encouragement. Why a fish? It was an acrostic; the first letter in each word of the Greek phrase, "Jesus Christ, Son of God, Savior" also spelled the word "fish" in Greek.*

We can encourage each other in following Jesus' teachings in a similar way.

Have participants pick *five* of the teachings above that may mean the most to them, or that are hardest for them to follow. Devise and memorize *hand signals* that correspond to the five teachings. Each person in the group can use the signals to encourage and remind each other over the next weeks.

End with the Lord's Prayer.

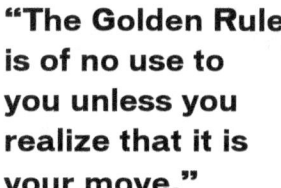

"The Golden Rule is of no use to you unless you realize that it is your move."

Mike Atkinson, youth leader

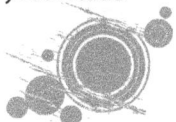

INSIGHTS FROM SCRIPTURE

This final series of teachings from the Sermon on the Mount focuses on religious practices, daily cares, and the journey that is God's Way:

- Perform religious practices (like giving to the poor, praying, and fasting) for God, not for public recognition.
- Trust God (more than money) for the things we need, and expect God to meet needs when asked.
- Jesus concludes with instruction for staying on course in the daily journey as disciples of the Way.

›› RELIGIOSITY VERSUS TRUE FAITHFULNESS

Giving to the poor, praying, and fasting were common religious practices among first-century Jews, dictated by the laws of Moses (or Torah). Jesus highlights them as three examples of how the *attitude* with which one fulfills these obligations is more important than the fulfillment itself (Douglas Hare, *Matthew*, Interpretation Series). Jesus specifically warns disciples against "performing" to impress other people. Seeking glory for religious practice is not the same as seeking to glorify God. Then Jesus says, in essence, "God knows what you're up to, and God knows the state of your heart when you fulfill your religious obligations, and will reward you accordingly."

But what about "letting your light shine," as per Matthew 5:16? In that passage, the "your" is plural, that is, it refers to the whole community! Gather together and be a beacon of hope! On the other hand, the "your" in Matthew 6 is singular, referring to individuals who may be seeking attention for good deeds that they alone have done as performance.

›› ECONOMIC SECURITY AND DAILY NEEDS

Jesus warns against hoarding earthly wealth, either out of greed or anxiety, and acknowledges the power that money can have over us: "Where your treasure is, there your heart will be also."

Jesus knows how hard it is to put away daily concerns of personal needs, but he also knows the danger of attaching human worth to the things one can collect. Get some

"It is ostentatiousness in personal piety that is criticized here: drawing public attention to almsgiving, praying in public places so as to be seen, and calling attention to one's fasting. Such people will have to be satisfied with public recognition as their reward. They will get no reward from God."

Daniel Harrington, S.J., *The Gospel of Matthew* in the series, *Sacra Pagina*.

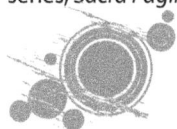

>> SEVEN DEADLY SOCIAL SINS

- Politics without principle
- Wealth without work
- Commerce without morality
- Pleasure without conscience
- Education without character
- Science without humanity
- Worship without sacrifice

Gandhi (quoted on a T-shirt)

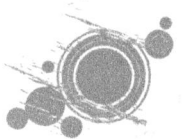

perspective, Jesus says. God created the world in which birds and lilies can thrive, and so can you live well here, if you give God free rein and don't let money rein you in.

It is appropriate that the teaching on judging comes on the heels of the teachings about daily living, for judging is a habit, a sign of a spirit of dis-ease. It also follows the passage on letting go of worry and releasing ourselves from the hold money has on us, all in response to divine generosity. When God has dealt so generously with us, how dare we be mean-spirited to others! He also warns that with judging, one needs to be prepared to get as good (or bad!) as one gives. "For with the judgment you make you will be judged, and the measure you give will be the measure you get" (7:2).

Finally, after a set of seemingly impossible demands concerning retaliation, loving enemies, the place of money and worry in our lives, and letting go of the habit of judging, Jesus offers an alternative: Go to God for help in carrying out these hard demands of discipleship. Douglas Hare sums up the "ask, seek, knock" passage: "Solely through tenacious dependence on God's graciousness can we deal graciously with those who provoke a negative reaction in us" (*Matthew*, Interpretation Series).

>> THE WAY TO FULFILLMENT

After a series of instructions in which "doing" is paramount (5:17–7:12), Jesus turns again, as in the Blessings (Beatitudes), to tough realities. Being a disciple will likely be hard, and will likely involve being misunderstood and rejected (the Greek word for "hard" in 7:14 means not so much *difficult* as it does *pressed upon*, or distressing). Jesus exhorts "ordinary" Christians to stay on the road of right living, and to ignore those whose fruits of living are not consistent with the ways of divine mercy.

Jesus concludes by encouraging his disciples to put what they have learned from him into practice. He says, "Everyone then who hears these words of mine and acts on them will be like a wise man who built his house on rock." These are a set of ethical instructions that far surpass the least-common-denominator brand of righteousness that fulfills the letter, but not the spirit, of the law.

The bottom line from these teachings is that righteous acts like giving, prayer, and fasting are for God, not public recognition. In addition, the more participants learn to know God, the more they will be able to understand and see that God loves us and will take care of us. Finally, in their journeys as disciples of Jesus, youth are to keep close on the path that Jesus lays out for them and to put what they learn from Jesus into practice.

>> LOOK AHEAD

Plan now if you will be using the **Extender Session** after this week's session.

>>> EXTENDER SESSION
(best used after Session 6)

MORE ON THE GOOD LIFE

>> Option A: Write your own homily
What would you write if you had a chance to say all the important things you want to say in one homily? What would you tell your parish about God? What would you say about how people should be living?

Invite participants to choose a scripture, find homily-writing helps online, and organize the points they want to make, and then give them free rein. Use the best ones, or synthesize them into one Gospel reflection for a youth mass.

>> Option B: Hillside prayer
Go to a hillside to practice the prayer and meditation techniques outlined in Sessions 2 and 4.

>> Option C: Practice mercy
Travel by twos or threes through your community, "practicing mercy," or random acts of kindness.

>> Option D: Poetic Blessings
Rewrite each of the Blessings (Beatitudes) in haiku. Traditional haiku, a Japanese poetry form, consists of three lines of five, seven, and five syllables, respectively. Ideally, a haiku presents a pair of contrasting images, one suggestive of time and place, the other a vivid but fleeting observation. Working together, they evoke mood and emotion. The poet does not comment on the connection but leaves the synthesis of the two images for the reader to perceive.

>> Materials needed and advance preparation

- Paper and pencils, or newsprint and markers laid out on tables
- Internet connection (Option A)
- Transportation planning and meditation instructions (Option B)
- Transportation planning and ideas for possible "random acts of kindness" (Option C)

Exploring tough questions facing youth today

CLUELESS AND CALLED
Discipleship and the Gospel of Mark

What does it take to be a disciple? This study of the Gospel of Mark focuses on the requirements for following Jesus' way and the abundant life that is ours as a result. (5 sessions)

DO MIRACLES HAPPEN?
Signs and Wonders in the Gospel of John

The greatest miracle, recorded in John 1:14 and 3:16, is the miracle of God's love that became flesh and lived among us. But John also included examples of what we more traditionally think of as miracles: the wonder of abundance from little; healing; signs of impossibility and faith; and the resurrection. (5 sessions)

DO THE RIGHT THING
Ethics Shaped by Faith

How do you know what's right and what's wrong? Even when you figure it out, the right thing is often the unpopular or unpleasant choice. This unit offers participants a clearer sense of what it means to claim a faith identity, a foundation that can help them sort out the gritty details of ethics shaped by faith. (6 sessions)

FIGHT RIGHT
A Christian Approach to Conflict Resolution

This unit will help youth understand conflict and its function. They will learn how they can be honest and loving, and explore how conflict can be used for positive results. They will also learn ways to enhance their communication skills. 1 Corinthians. (5 sessions)

GOD IS A WARRIOR?
Violence in the Bible

The Bible challenges us to be reconciled to one another and work for justice. So what do we do with the stories that seem to condone violence or even encourage it? A discussion of issues in the Old and New Testaments. (6 sessions)

HOW DO YOU KNOW?
Wisdom in the Bible

Wisdom literature teaches us that we gain knowledge of the world, ourselves, and God through experience and observation. This unit provides practical, hands-on wisdom to help young people avoid life's snares and grow closer to God. Proverbs, Job, Ecclesiastes. (5 sessions)

HOW TO BE A TRUE FRIEND
The Bible Reveals Friendship's Heart

To be a friend takes skill. Help youth discover the secrets of friendship through various stories from the Old and New Testament. (6 sessions)

HOW TO READ THE BIBLE
Building Skills for Bible Study

What kind of book is the Bible? What does this book mean to me? This unit looks at the Bible as revelation, as history, as literature. Selected scripture. (5 sessions)

KEEPING THE GARDEN
A Faith Response to God's Creation

If Christians believe that God made the world, we do not need any more compelling reason to care for it than that God has handed us a treasure to hold and protect. This unit gets beyond trendy environmentalism and challenges youth to see environmental awareness as a religious issue. Genesis. (6 sessions)

MANTRAS, MENORAHS, AND MINARETS
Encountering Other Faiths

How is Christianity different from other faiths? Why do others believe the way they do? This study can give youth a new appreciation for the uniqueness of Jesus. Selected scripture. (5 sessions)

SALT, LIGHT, AND THE GOOD LIFE
The Beatitudes and the Sermon on the Mount

What can youth expect in a life of discipleship? This unit explores the Sermon on the Mount under four main sections: the Beatitudes, Salt and Light, Jesus and the Law, and Heavenly Teachings. Matthew 5. (6 sessions)

A SPECK IN THE UNIVERSE
The Bible on Self-Esteem and Peer Pressure

Discover God's unconditional love and acceptance of all people. This study will show positive ways to have one's life make a difference, and help youth find ways to resist negative peer pressure and turn it into positive action. (6 sessions)

THE RADICAL REIGN
Parables of Jesus

Jesus used parables to reveal what the kingdom of God is like, and how God relates to us. This study highlights how the parables reveal God's reign as radically different from the world we live in, and what that means for the Christian life. (6 sessions)

TESTING THE WATERS
Basic Tenets of Faith

Discover the biblical roots for the central Christian concepts of covenant, community, and baptism. This short course is a way to test the (baptismal) waters of Christianity before diving in, or review the basics for those who already have. (6 sessions)

WHO IS GOD?
Engaging the Mystery

God is beyond human comprehension, yet desires to be known. These sessions focus on the way we get clues about and glimpses of God from the Bible, God's creation, and church tradition. Selected scripture. (5 sessions)

www.ingramcontent.com/pod-product-compliance
Lightning Source LLC
Chambersburg PA
CBHW080326170426
43193CB00030B/2857